Art Deco Designs

CD-ROM and Book

DOVER PUBLICATIONS, INC.

Mineola, New York

The CD-ROM on the inside back cover contains all of the images shown in the book. There is no installation necessary. Just insert the CD into your computer and call the images into your favorite software (refer to the documentation with your software for further instructions). Each image has been scanned at 600 dpi and saved in six different formats—BMP, EPS, GIF, JPEG, PICT, and TIFF. The JPEG and GIF files—the most popular graphics file types used on the Web—are Internet-ready.

The "Images" folder on the CD contains a number of different folders. All of the TIFF images have been placed in one folder, as have all of the PICT, all of the EPS, etc. The images in each of these folders are identical except for file format. Every image has a unique file name in the following format: xxx.xxx. The first 3 or 4 characters of the file name, before the period, correspond to the number printed with the image in the book. The last 3 characters of the file name, after the period, refer to the file format. So, 001.TIF would be the first file in the TIFF folder.

Also included on the CD-ROM is Dover Design Manager, a simple graphics editing program for Windows that will allow you to view, print, crop, and rotate the images.

For technical support, contact:
Telephone: 1 (617) 249-0245
Fax: 1 (617) 249-0245
Email: dover@artimaging.com
Internet: **http://www.dovertechsupport.com**
The fastest way to receive technical support is via email or the Internet.

Bibliographical Note

Art Deco Designs CD-ROM and Book is a new work, first published by Dover Publications, Inc., in 2005.

Dover Electronic Clip Art®

International Standard Book Number: 0-486-99663-8

Manufactured in the United States of America
Dover Publications, Inc., 31 East 2nd Street, Mineola, N.Y. 11501

PLATE 1. 001. Otto Arpke; magazine cover design. **002.** Design for an apertif advertisement. **003.** Robert Bonfils; poster for the Paris 1925 Exhibition. **004.** Heinemann; detail from an art printers mark. **005.** Rene Paul Chambellan and Jacques Delamarre; copper repoussé frieze, Chanin Building, New York; 1929. **006.** Austin Cooper; detail from poster. **007.** Naitō Haruji; cast bronze wall clock; Japanese; 1927. **008.** Jacques Lipchitz; "Woman with Gazelles," bronze; Lithuanian; 1911. **009.** William Metzig; trademark design. **010.** Jean Carlu; magazine cover for "Le plaisir de vivre."

PLATE 2. 011. Yolande Mas; design for a cigarette case. **012.** Otto Wolfe; logo for his own services. **013.** Erté; costume design for Gaby Deslys; 1918. **014.** Kiyomizu Rokubei VI; earthenware vase, painted in enamels; Japanese; 1933. **015.** Decoration from a page of *The Pearl;* Japanese. **016.** J Fenneker; design for the film, "Der Frauen-Konig."

PLATE 3. 017. Trias (Rolf Frey); ad for pearls. **018.** Pendant; probably German or French; ca. 1925–30. **019.** Yolande Mas; design for a cigarette lighter. **020.** Walentin Zietara; design for cigarette ad. **021.** Design for Atelier Trias. **022.** Fromenti; fashion illustration. **023.** Otto Poertzel; "Butterfly Dancers," ivory carving. **024.** Leon Benigni; fashion illustration.

025

026

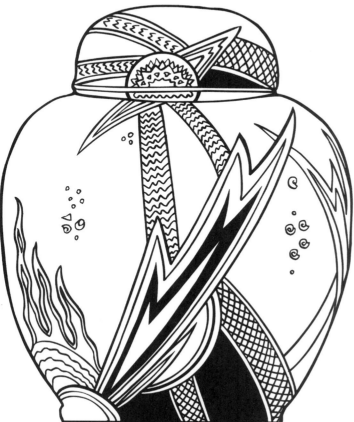

027

028

PLATE 4. 025. Lee Lawrie; relief above the door at the RCA building, Rockefeller Center, New York; 1931. **026.** Tadeusz Gronowski; poster for Fruzinski confectionery; Polish; ca. 1925. **027.** Enoch Boulton; earthenware ginger jar painted in enamels and gilt; British; 1928–30. **028.** E.A. Seguy; French.

029

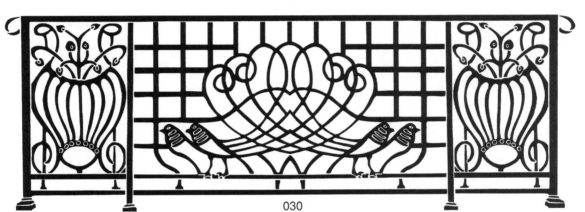

030

031

PLATE 5. 029. Mosaic panel from the Westinghouse Pavilion at the 1933 Century of Progress Exposition in Chicago; American; 1933. **030.** Fonderies Du Val D'Osne, ironworker; balustrade. **031.** A. Armitage (OA); ad design.

033

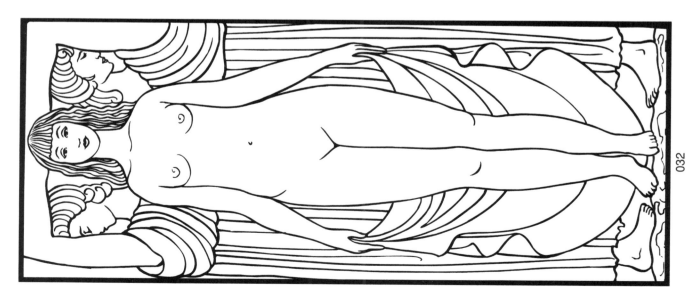

032

PLATE 6. **032.** Bouvard, architect; sculpture by Bouraine and Le Faguays; bas relief for the Pavilion of the City of Paris. **033.** Jeanne Paquin; "Chimere," beaded silk evening gown; French; 1925.

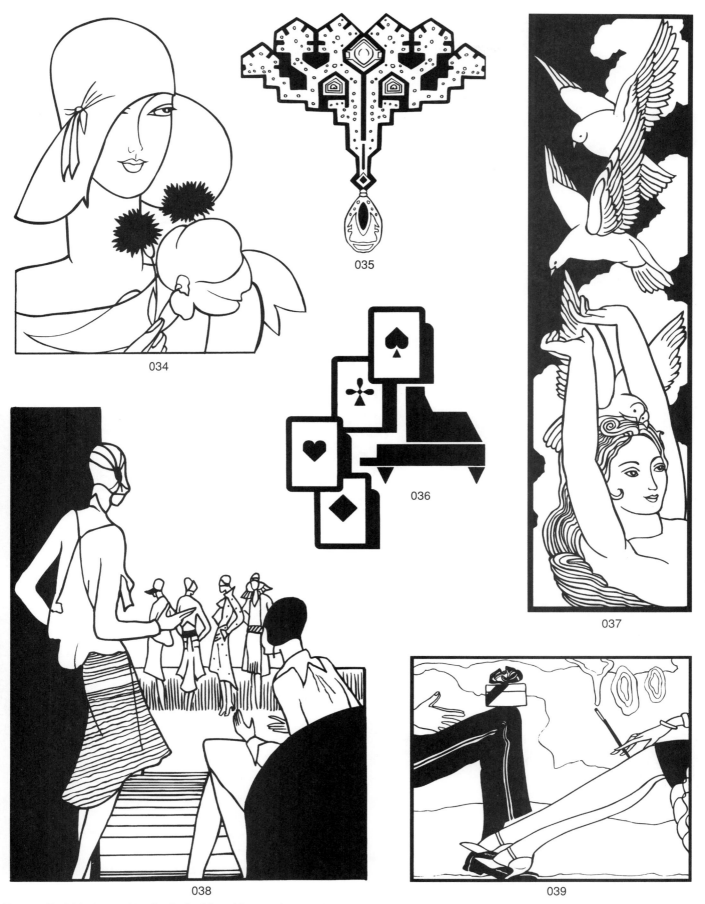

PLATE 7. 034. Leon Benigni; fashion illustration and magazine cover. **035.** Pendant; probably French or German; 1925–30. **036.** Georg Goedecker, typographic artist; design for his services. **037.** Jean Dupas; detail from "Les Perruches," oil on canvas; French; 1925. **038.** Lotte Wernekink; fashion illustration. **039.** Design for a hosiery company.

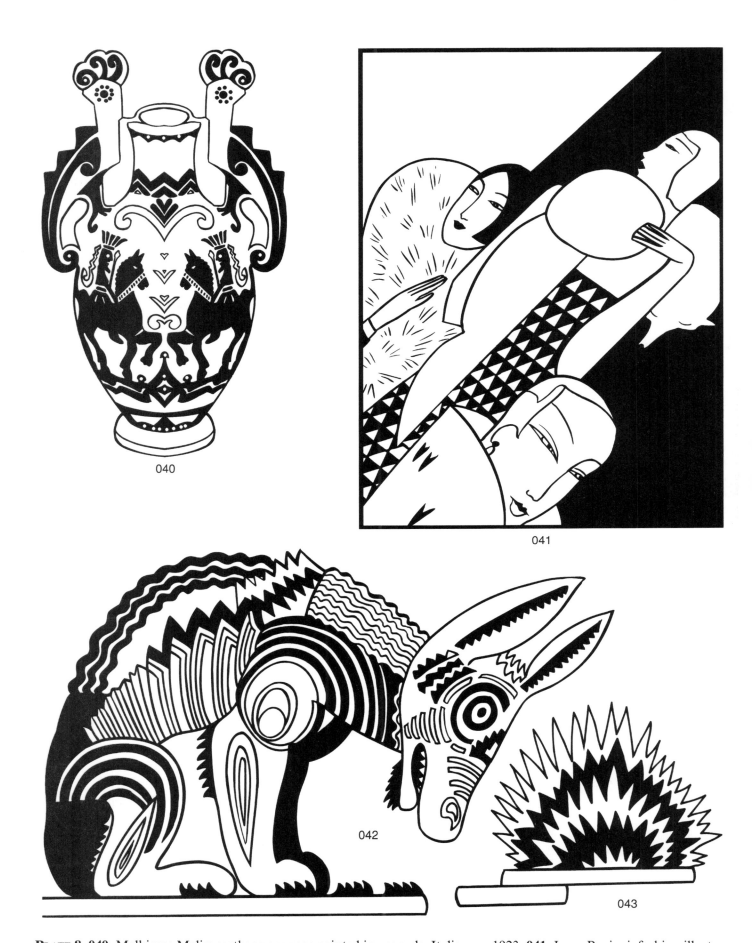

PLATE 8. 040. Melkiorre Melis; earthenware vase painted in enamels; Italian; ca.1923. **041.** Leon Benigni; fashion illustration. **042 & 043.** Jacques-Emile Ruhlmann, Jean Dunand, and Jean Lambert-Rucki; decoration from black lacquered cabinet with incised silver decoration; French; 1925.

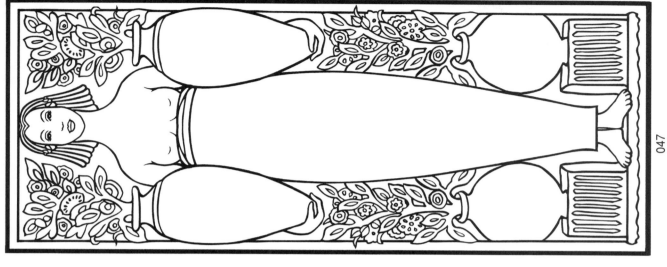

047

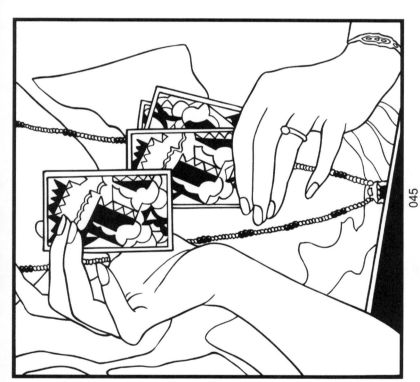

045

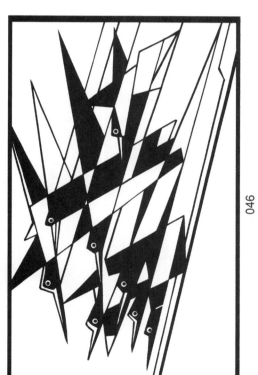

046

044

PLATE 9. **044.** Pattern from book by Thomas and Darcy. **045.** Jean Carlu; playing card design. **046.** Edward McNight Kauffer; "Soaring to Success!" color lithograph; The Early Bird poster, the *Daily Herald;* American; 1918. **047.** Gaillard, architect; bas relief for a tavern.

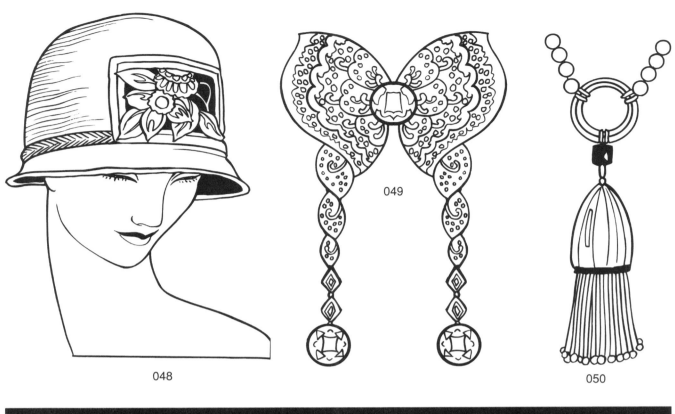

048

049

050

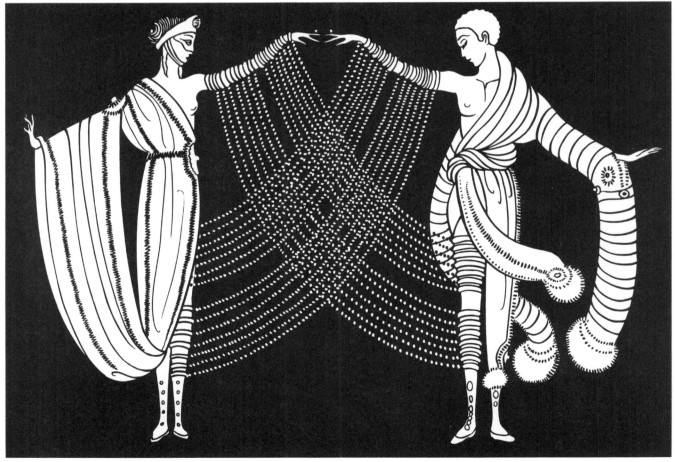

051

PLATE 10. 048. Kilpin Ltd.; mannequin wearing pink straw cloche with appliqué trim; British; ca. 1925. **049.** Brooch; probably French or German; 1925–30. **050.** Georges Fouquet; tassel necklace of frosted rock crystal, nylon, onyx, and enamel; French; 1925. **051.** Erté; plate from *L'Illustration;* Paris; 1926.

PLATE 11. 052. Pablo Picasso; costume for the Chinese conjurer in the Massine ballet, *Parade;* Spanish; ca. 1917. **053.** Scarab brooch inspired by the Egyptian revival of the 1920s. **054.** Arthur Carlsson Percy; earthenware tureen painted in enamels; Swedish; 1930. **055.** Advertising design from Diversified Art and Engraving Services. **056.** Paul Manship; "Europa and the Bull," bronze; American; 1924.

PLATE 12. 057. Narotamdas Bhau; piece from a silver and celluloid tea service; Indian; ca. 1920–29. **058.** Bouvard, architect; sculpture by Bouraine and Le Faguays; bas relief for the Pavilion of the City of Paris. **059.** Marcel Bergue, iron worker; detail of console. **060.** Gerhard Henning; "The Chinese Bride," painted porcelain; Danish; ca. 1922.

PLATE 13. 061. Design for brooch. **062 & 064.** Pendants; probably French or German; 1925–30. **063.** Pattern from book by Thomas and Darcy. **065.** Leon Benigni; magazine cover. **066.** Trias (Rolf Frey); perfume ad.

067

068

069

070

PLATE 14. 067. Edgar Brandt, ironworker; detail from interior grillwork, Pavillon du Collectionneur. **068.** Jeanne Paquin; "Chimere," beaded silk evening gown; French; 1925. **069.** Edgar Brandt; wrought iron firescreen. **070.** Shawl of silk, velvet and lamé; French; ca. 1925.

PLATE 15. 071. Josef Hoffmann; gilded metal bowl; Austrian; ca. 1924. **072.** Jewelry clasp; probably French or German; 1925–30. **073.** Paul Colin; "Le tumulte Noire," plate depicting Josephine Baker. **074.** Edgar Brandt, ironworker; detail of door.

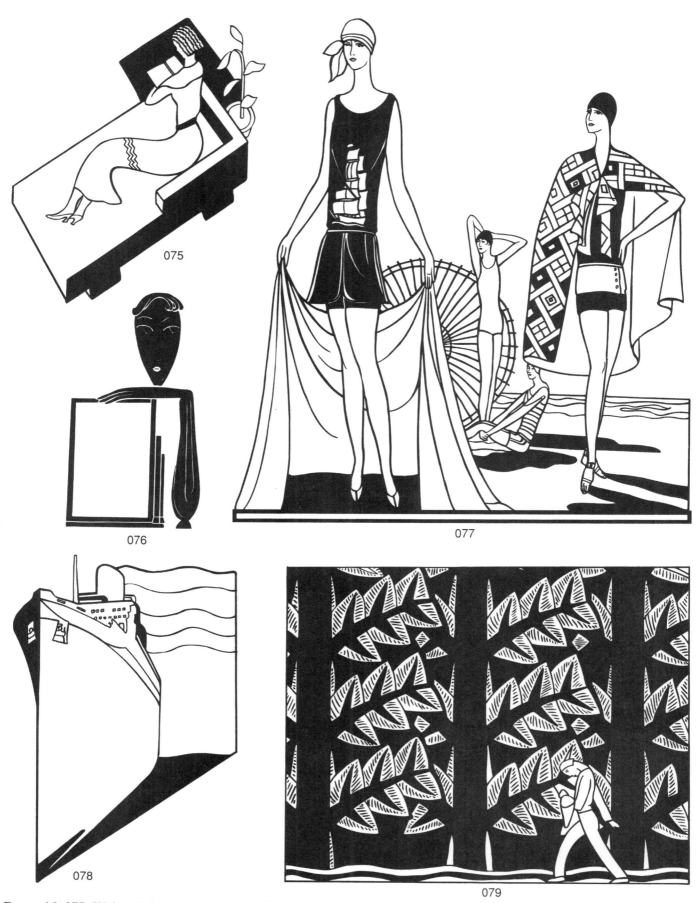

PLATE 16. 075. Walter Reimer; poster design for an interior decoration show. 076. Franz Hagenauer; brass and mirrored glass; Austrian; ca. 1925. 077. Henri Mercier; fashion illustration. 078. J.R.Tooby; Canadian Pacific Railway poster, color lithograph; British; ca. 1931–40. 079. Theyre Lee-Elliott; from book jacket design for *Africa Notwithstanding* by Kenneth Granville Bradley, color lithograph; London; 1930.

080

081

082

083

PLATE 17. 080. Joseph Binder; poster design. **081.** Marc Erol; lamp. **082.** Pattern from book by Thomas and Darcy. **083.** Border pattern.

PLATE 18. 084. Pendant; probably French or German; 1925–30. **085.** Marcel Groupy; enameled and gilded blown glass vase; French; ca. 1925. **086.** Boucheron; corsage ornament; French; 1925. **087.** Edgar Brandt, ironworker; fireplace screen. **088.** Cartier; jeweled vanity case; French; 1925.

089

090

091

092

093

094

PLATE 19. 089. Jean Schwartz, ironworker; grillwork for an apartment block. **090.** William Metzig; trademark. **091.** Bracelet; probably French or German; 1925–30. **092.** Ilonka Karasz; fabric for Lesher-Whiuman Co. **093.** Pattern from book by Thomas and Darcy. **094.** Gregory Brown; roller printed cotton furnishing fabric; British; 1922.

095

096

097

098

PLATE 20. 095. Joel and Jan Martel; "The Island of Avalon," stone carving. **096.** Georges Fouquet; brooch with white gold, blue enamel and diamonds; French; ca. 1931. **097.** Auguste Lazo; stoneware tile with Mayan motifs; made by American Encaustic Tiling Co.; 1928. **098.** Fortunato Depero; design for American *Vogue;* watercolor on paper; Italian; 1929.

PLATE 21. 099. Robert Cheveux; magazine cover. **100.** Pendant; probably French or German; 1925–30. **101.** Atelier Martine; block printed satin; French; 1919. **102.** E.B. Ulreich; page decoration. **103.** Georges Lepape.

PLATE 22. 104. Victor Schreckengost; glazed porcelain punch bowl with sgraffito decoration; American; 1931. **105 & 107.** Enameled perfume bottles. **106.** Georges Fouquet; brooch with white gold, blue enamel, and diamonds; French. **108.** Clarice Cliff; Coffee pot, cup, and saucer.

PLATE 23. 109. René Buthaud; "Europa and the Bull," ceramic vase. **110.** Fromenti; ad for a comb. **111.** Jewelry, probably French or German; 1925–30. **112.** Lydia Bush-Brown Head; "Temple of the Mayan Indians," silk; American; 1926.

113   114   115

116

PLATE 24. 113. Joseph Binder; design for Borax ad. **114.** Trias (Rolf Frey); ad for a nightclub, "Pavilion Mascott." **115.** Gérard Sandoz; "Guitar," pendant of frosted crystal, labradorite, lacquer, pink and white gold, and black silk; French; ca. 1928. **116.** Jean Dupas; detail from "Les Perruches," oil on canvas; French; 1925.

PLATE 25. 117. For a printer ad. **118.** William Metzig design. **119.** Enameled brooch. **120.** Zhang Zhengyu; "Kuangwu" (Crazy wild dancing); from *Shanghai Huabao;* 1929. **121.** Louis Süe and André Mare; bronze mantel clock. **122.** Pin; probably French or German; 1925–30.

PLATE 26. 123. Theyre Lee-Elliott; design for jacket of Georgette Heyer novel; London, printed in USA; 1929. **124.** René Buthaud; stoneware vase; French; 1920. **125.** Gio Ponti; "La conversazione classica," porcelain vase; Italian; 1927. **126.** Calvin Picone; design for a commercial art film.

PLATE 27. 127. Pendant; probably French or German; 1925–30. **128.** Cartier; pendant, diamonds and onyx in open-back platinum setting; French; 1913. **129.** Jean Dunand; decorated lacquerware medallion; 1927. **130.** Necklace; probably French or German; 1925–30. **131.** Paul Manship; "The Flight of Europa," bronze; American; 1925.

PLATE 28. 132 & 134. Leon Benigni; fashion illustration and magazine cover. **133.** Pin; probably French or German; 1925–30. **135.** Raoul Dufy; printed linen furnishing fabric; French; ca. 1920. **136.** Henri Le Monnier; ad for gloves. **137.** Yamazaki Kakutarō; jewelry box of lacquer on wood; Japanese; 1934.

PLATE 29. 138. Bracelet; probably French or German; 1925–30. **139.** Pattern from book by Thomas and Darcy. **140.** Cassandre; ad for a cap. **141.** Carl Schupig; trademark. **142.** Fortunato Depero; "Serada," wool tapestry; Italian; 1920. **143.** Bagues Freres, ironworker; door.

PLATE 30. 144. Bracelet; probably French or German; 1925–30. **145.** Clarice Cliff; ceramic wall plaque depicting a Russian couple, inspired by Diaghilev's ballets. **146.** Jean Carlu; magazine cover for *Vanity Fair*. **147.** Designer unknown; book jacket for Harvey Fergusson's *Hot Saturday;* London, printed in New York; 1926.

148

149

150

PLATE 31. 148. Marcel Bergue, ironworker; fireplace screen. **149.** Pattern from book by Thomas and Darcy. **150.** Rene Paul Chambellan and Jacques Delamarre; copper repoussé frieze on the Chanin Building, New York; 1929.

153

152

151

PLATE 32. 151. Jean Dunand; lacquered brass vase; French; 1931. 152. Edgar Brandt, ironworker; "Les Cigognes d' Alsace," panel for a lift cage; lacquer and metal on wood; French. 153. Edgar Brandt; interior gate of patinated and gilt wrought ironwork.

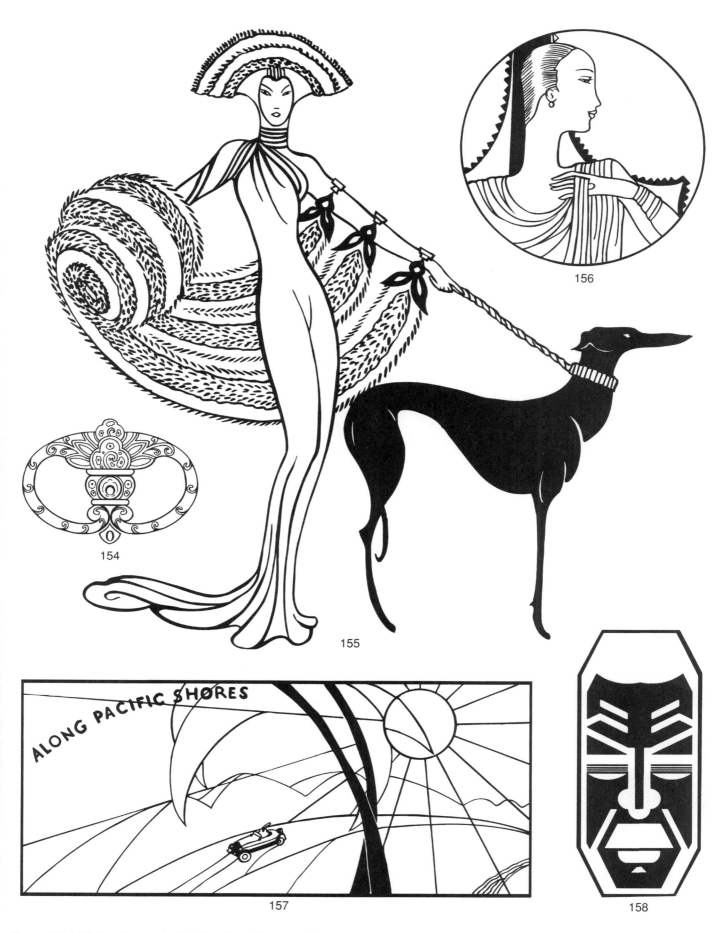

PLATE 33. 154. Jewelry; probably French or German; 1925–3. **155.** Erté; "Woman Dressed in Black"; 1930s. **156.** Leon Benigni; fashion illustration. **157.** Maurice del Mue (OA); design for travel poster. **158.** Georg Goedecker; typographic design.

PLATE 34. 159. "Maga" studio; design for beer advertisement. **160.** Design for a coupon. **161.** Decorative mask on the facade of the Pavilion of the City of Paris. **162.** Tea service, earthenware painted in enamels; British; 1931–35. **163.** Poster design.

164

165

166

167

PLATE 35. 164. Raoul Dufy; "La danse," printed linen furnishing fabric; French; 1925. **165.** Cassandre; design for a poster advertising an atomizer. **166.** Alfred Tolmer; plate from *Mise en Page: The Theory and Practice of Layout;* London; 1931. **167.** Pattern from book by Thomas and Darcy.

PLATE 36. 168. Jewelry; probably French or German; 1925–30. **169.** Bracelet; probably French or German; 1925–30. **170 & 173.** Pattern from book by Thomas and Darcy. **171 & 174.** Georg Goedecker; typographic design. **172.** Darcy; design for Saks Fifth Ave women's apparel.

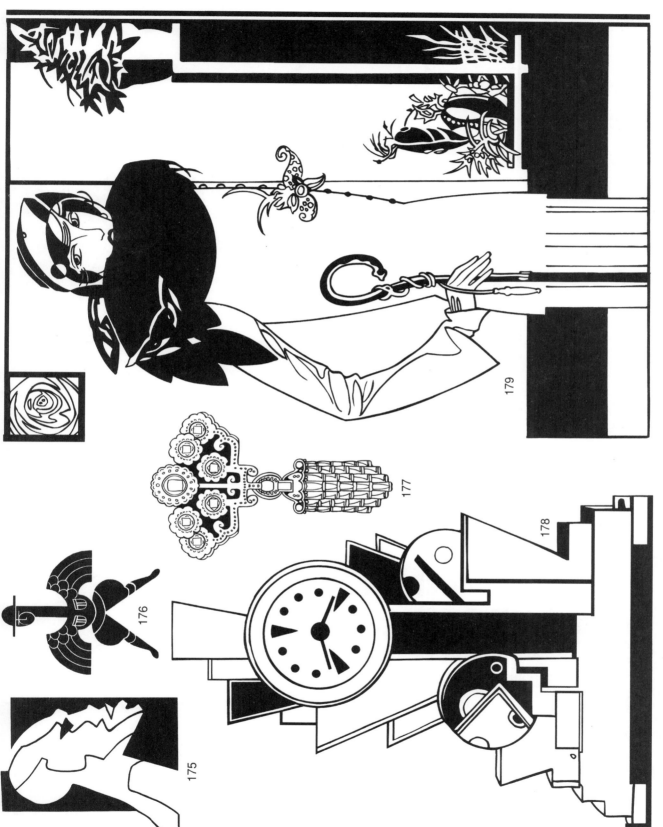

PLATE 37. 175. Theyre Lee-Elliott; from book jacket design for Kenneth Granville Bradley's *Africa Notwithstanding,* color lithograph; London; 1932. **176.** William Metzig; typographic design. **177.** Pendant; probably French or German; 1925–30. **178.** Jean Golden; clock of silvered bronze with enamel; French; 1928. **179.** Julius Klinger; design for a printer "Chwala's Druck."

PLATE **38. 180.** Wilhelm Kåge; decoration from an Argenta vase of stoneware inlaid with silver; Swedish; ca. 1930. **181.** Advertising design for a manicuring product. **182.** Jean Broome-Norton; "Abundance," bronze; Australian; 1934.

183

184

185

PLATE 39. 183. Edgar Brandt, ironworker; fireplace screen. **184.** Lajos Kozma; carved and gilded wood mirror; Hungarian; ca. 1920. **185.** C.A. Angrave; design for motoring.

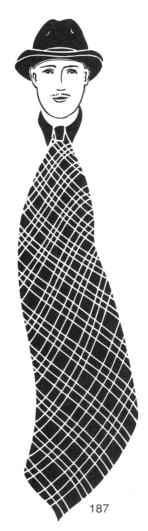

PLATE 40. 186. Pattern from book by Thomas and Darcy. **187.** Alfons Plasil; advertisement for "Old Boy" ties. **188.** Edgar Brandt, ironworker; fireplace screen. **189.** Design for a printer.

PLATE 41. 190. Stained glass window; executed after designs by A.D. Copier; made in the Netherlands. **191.** Personal trademark by G.B. Jensen. **192.** Pattern from book by Thomas and Darcy. **193.** Design for a commercial art studio. **194.** Paul Manship; "Dancer and the Gazelles," bronze; American; 1916. **195.** Cassandre; design for a film daily.

PLATE 42. 196. Robert Bonfils; decoration on inside cover of Henri de Regnier's *Les Rencontres de M. Breot;* Paris; 1919. **197.** Enameled jewelry. **198.** Robert Foster; magazine cover for American Printer; 1928. **199.** Hans Ibe; poster advertisement for optical firm. **200.** Edward McKnight Kauffer; cotton bale label, color lithograph; American; 1925.

PLATE 43. 201. Georges Lepape; cover for *British Vogue,* showing a model wearing a Sonia Delaunay dress; 1925. **202.** Fromenti; illustration for hair ornament. **203.** Pattern from book by Thomas and Darcy. **204.** Rene Paul Chambellan; wrought iron and bronze entrance gates to the executive suite of the Canin Building, New York; American; 1928. **205.** Design by E.A. Seguy.

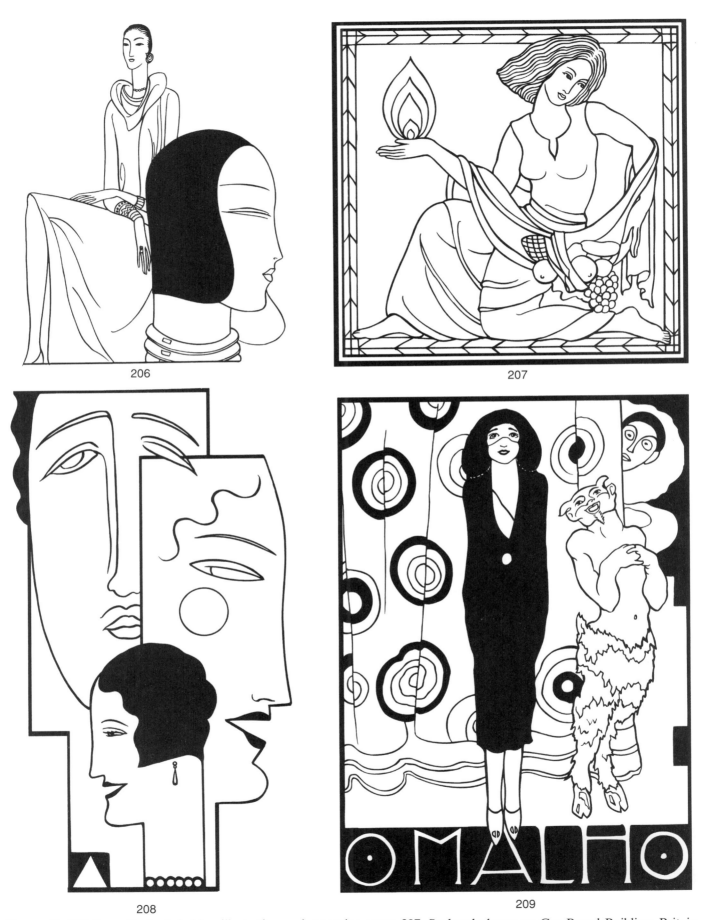

206

207

208

209

PLATE 44. 206. Leon Benigni; fashion illustration and magazine cover. **207.** Sculpted plaque on Gas Board Building; Britain. **208.** Jean Carlu; poster art for a performer, Pepe Bonafe. **209.** Emiliano di Cavalcanti; cover of *O Malho;* Latin American; 1919.

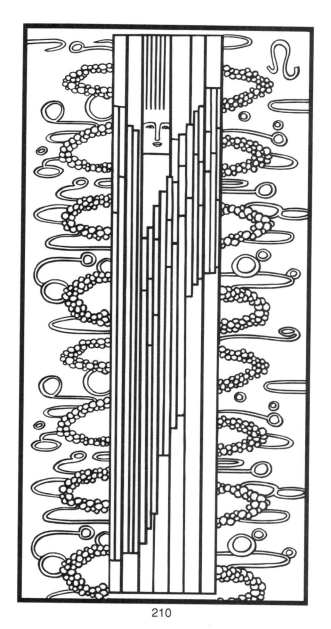

210

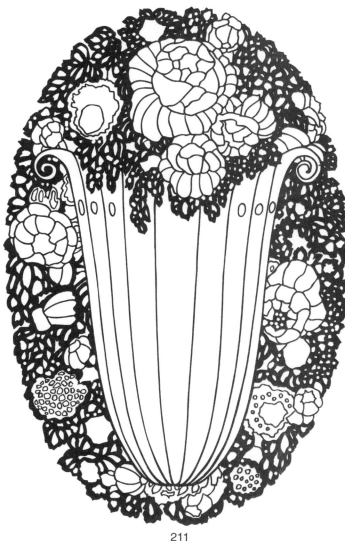

211

212

213

PLATE 45. 210. Napier Waller; detail from "Ceres," stained glass and lead Leicke Window; Australia; 1935. **211.** Jacques-Emile Ruhlmann; frontice art on lacquered rosewood corner cabinet, ivory and rare woods; French; 1916. **212.** Exhibition poster, *La Croisiere noire au Louvre*; French; 1926. **213.** Pattern from book by Thomas and Darcy.

Index